Bernard Davey's Mourne

Ten Walks in Mourne

with the

Weatherman

Cottage
Publications

This book of walks through the Mourne area is aimed at the walker who wants to spend a day absorbing the beauty of the region, as well as getting some useful exercise. The book is beautifully put together by my former colleague Bernard Davey, who has used his comfortable style of communication to take the reader on a series of delightful walks. The photographs, maps and drawings are especially good and whet the appetite for more. There are snippets on flora and fauna as well as information of historical interest and, of course, a whole chapter on the weather.

Whether you tackle one or more of the walks you will feel invigorated and well informed.

Happy walking,

*...I love to go a wandering
along the mountain track......*

Contents

Introduction

While I could not be described as a Son of Mourne I can claim to be a Grandson of Mourne. My maternal grandmother, Mary Anne Harrison was born and reared in Ballyveaghmore, Ballymartin, in the shadow of Slieve Binnian. The name Harrison hails from Northeast England. Mary Anne's father William, came from Newcastle-upon-Tyne to buy ponies for the coal-mining industry. He fell in love with a Mourne maid, Elizabeth Cunningham, married and stayed. They lived off Sabbath Hill Road in a two storey dwelling known as 'The Big House'. The house itself was not large by modern day standards but it was much bigger than the surrounding stone cottages. Unfortunately, like many older dwellings in Mourne, it has succumbed to the ravages of

The Big House at Sabbath Hill Road

time and neglect. The Harrisons were well off but unfortunately William and Elizabeth died when the family were still young, so Mary Anne, her sister Bridget and three brothers George, Edward and Joseph had to fend for themselves from an early age. Bridget and Joseph were twins and still babes in the cradle at the time.

Mother and Father, Newcastle 1956

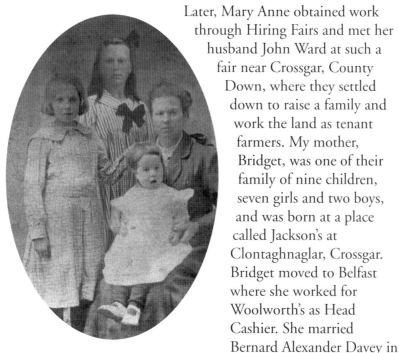

Ward family: Grandmother Mary Anne with three of her daughters L to R Margaret Theresa, Bridget (my mother) and youngest, Ellen Jane.

Later, Mary Anne obtained work through Hiring Fairs and met her husband John Ward at such a fair near Crossgar, County Down, where they settled down to raise a family and work the land as tenant farmers. My mother, Bridget, was one of their family of nine children, seven girls and two boys, and was born at a place called Jackson's at Clontaghnaglar, Crossgar. Bridget moved to Belfast where she worked for Woolworth's as Head Cashier. She married Bernard Alexander Davey in Belfast in 1936. They had six children, four boys and two girls and I was born on 29th March 1943. While my mother was giving birth in the back bedroom of a terraced house in Belfast, across the Irish Sea a Mrs. Major was also giving birth to a son whom she named John. John Major, of course, became the British Prime Minister, during my time as a TV weather presenter. I often kid people that I was named after the two British generals, Bernard Montgomery and Lord Alexander who were engaged in the Battle of El Alamein which was won at that time. However, since I was the third son, tradition had already decreed that I was named after my father.

Newcastle became the family's favourite holiday destination from as early as 1948 when I was five and in 1957 my mother fulfilled her dream of having a country cottage, when South Cottage, King Street, was purchased for the princely sum of three hundred and fifty pounds. It was here that I practiced my do-it-yourself skills as her 'dream' was in great need of repair.

*South Cottage,
King Street*

In 1962 I left school to join the Meteorological Office. My first position was at the old Belfast Airport, Nutt's Corner, as an Assistant Scientific Officer. It was a mobile grade and thus started a career that would take me to several locations in the United Kingdom and overseas, including Germany and Libya, where incidentally I, like many others, had to leave hastily when Colonel Gadaffi came to power in the 'September Revolution' of 1969. The Americans were given three months to leave and the British six months. As part of the orderly evacuation I departed for the United Kingdom by air courtesy of a Royal Air Force VC10. My final six years were spent as a Weather Presenter for the BBC in London. I was the thirty first presenter and joined the illustrious team of Bill Giles, Ian McCaskill, Michael Fish and John Kettley. Weather presentation on TV was an expanding empire. In 1987 I arrived and made the team up to five, while today the number of presenters has increased four-fold. By the time my career came to an abrupt end I was a Senior Scientific Officer and Deputy Head of the BBC Weather Centre.

In 1992 I was diagnosed with Multiple Sclerosis (MS). MS was no surprise as I already suspected the diagnosis, due to the many symptoms I was experiencing, so I decided to quit TV while I was ahead and on 31st December 1993 I accepted medical retirement. June 1994 saw me moving back to Newcastle, Northern Ireland where I bought an old Victorian house on the sea front. An added bonus was establishing contact with several unknown cousins dotted around the Mourne area.

Walking the Mournes, often with Charly the family yellow Labrador, has kept me in a positive frame of mind and I have thoroughly enjoyed writing this book. I would never admit to being an expert on any subject, even the weather, but I hope I have given you an overview of the region. While I have concentrated on the East Mournes I will become more familiar with the rest of Mourne and Slieve Croob in the future. Organising transport for walks can be difficult, especially when travelling cross-country. For this reason I have devised five circular walks; Numbers 1, 2, 6, 8 and 10. Number 7 is easily managed during the summer months by catching the Silent Valley bus from Newcastle around ten o'clock in the morning. The other four walks will need a little more organisation. Finally, I trust you will enjoy reading the book in the comfort of your home and, if you plan to embark on any of the walks, then the Route Cards provided will help guide you on your way.

Slieve Donard

I first climbed Slieve Donard with my brother Seany when I was in my early teens. We took the most direct route possible through the fire break at King Street, up Millstone Mountain and then to the top of Donard. After a few minutes to savour the summit, it was helter-skelter back to the bottom, collapsing in a heap but still managing to indulge in self-congratulations between the gasps for breath. We dusted ourselves down before returning to my aunt's house at 95 King Street, where we were staying on holiday. Seany swore me to secrecy, as there would have been hell to pay if my parents had found out where we had been. They wouldn't have been worried about me but Seany, who was an epileptic. He died when he was thirty years old.

Some twenty years later I attempted a re-run of Slieve Donard with my son and niece, only to be thwarted at the last stages by cloud spilling over the summit, on what was up to then a fine summer's day. Within minutes we were enveloped in cloud or fog, with visibility down to 20 yards. We had to beat a hasty retreat, taking care to bear a little right, as I was afraid of falling into the quarry on Thomas's Mountain. One does naturally bear right when lost in fog and go round in circles, just like the poor legionnaire lost in the desert. We did over compensate, eventually reaching the main road at the Bloody Bridge a few miles away from our starting point. After that lesson in mountain climbing and meteorology I stick to the safer, recognised route along the Glen River which, to be honest, is much more interesting, with plenty of places to pause and reflect. You are also more likely to meet people from near and far.

Visitors to Newcastle can't help but be immediately impressed by the Mourne Mountains, as they sweep majestically up from the Irish Sea, with Slieve Donard, the

With constant companion Charly

highest mountain in Northern Ireland at 2,796 feet (850 metres), standing sentinel over the surrounding area. Anyone with a reasonable level of fitness should be able to complete this challenging walk in less than five hours and they will be amply rewarded for their efforts. It is the most popular walk in all the Mournes, not because it is the most beautiful or the most spectacular, but because it is the highest and anyone worth their salt wants to impress their friends along the promenade by telling them, "I've been up there!" Apart from that, the route beside the Glen River makes it very accessible for visitors, holidaymakers and residents alike. Just as a matter of interest, did you know that Mount Everest at 29,028 feet is only ten times higher than Slieve Donard? I say only, but that converts to an awesome five and a half miles.

Donard car park is the starting point. Above the arch at the entrance is the date 1951, marking the year the park was opened to the public by the then Newcastle District Council. Before that the land belonged to the Annesley family, who originated in Nottinghamshire and first settled in Castlewellan in 1758, when Newcastle was no more than a village. It wasn't until 1830 that Newcastle began its rise to fame, when the third Earl Annesley built a marine residence, Donard Lodge, on the slopes of Thomas's Mountain and surrounded it with an extensive demesne.

The Glen River justifying its alternative name

Much of this walk is alongside the Glen River, thought by many to be the prettiest of the Mourne rivers. The cascades and waterfalls are particularly scenic, especially the last few hundred metres before levelling out at Donard Park. I often come here to watch the torrents of frothing water crashing down when the river is in spate, after heavy rains. This is probably the reason the river is also known as White River. This area is most restful, particularly in winter when the peace and quiet are conducive to contemplation and prayer. When I married in June 1965 I came to Newcastle for my honeymoon and my wife Teresa and I spent some time walking in the demesne admiring the trees and rhododendrons. Despite a certain amount of neglect the area still supports a healthy level of flora and fauna.

The path beside the Glen River is easily identified and you enter Donard Wood where the climb begins in earnest. The popularity of this route is soon obvious because generations of walkers have worn away the soil to reveal a tangle of tree roots. Donard Bridge, which was built in 1835, is the first stopping point as it provides a fantastic platform for viewing the waterfalls and cascades. The bridge was built as the main crossing point for access to Donard Lodge, which is sadly nothing more than a pile of overgrown rubble. I've seen grey herons fishing here so that's a fair indication that the river supports a few trout. While the first time visitor to the river will want to stop at every vantage point as they continue the upward journey, they should take care not to step too close to unguarded precipices or walk on the wet stones. It is worth keeping an eye out for the waterfall that disappears into the tiny Hermit's Glen. It's recognisable by a warning sign, a large overhanging oak tree and what appears to be a stone grotto or shelter. Many years ago, Newcastle got its water directly from the Glen River and there is still evidence of this in various places in Donard Wood. Just before you reach the next bridge, which is known as the Glen River or Craignagore Bridge, you can see a large pool with a grille,

Glen River Bridge

Slieve Croob and Castlewellan from Donard Wood

through which water used to be diverted. At one time the river also generated electricity for the town. After a long walk, especially if returning this way, I find it very refreshing to bathe my feet in one of the pools of icy cold water. During hot summers, when Newcastle is chock-a-block with visitors, every pool along this first stretch is in great demand. A short walk northwards along the forest path unveils a splendid view of Newcastle and the surrounding countryside. In years to come, this view will become obscured as the saplings mature into fully grown trees.

By the time you reach the third and last bridge, Sonny's Bridge, you have climbed 600 feet and will certainly want to get your second wind if you haven't already done so. I've been told that this is a good place for spotting Long Eared Owls, though you are unlikely to see them in broad daylight. From here the mountain gate is visible and by venturing onto the open mountains you experience for the first time a sense of wilderness. I should point out that once

you pass through the gate you exit Donard Wood and enter National Trust property. In 1991 the National Trust purchased a large slice of Slieve Donard for £500,000.

A short distance upstream, on the other side of the river, lies the Ice House which is actually an ancient refrigerator and was very recently restored by the National Trust. Workers from the Annesley estate would cut away chunks of

The Mountain Gate and Eagle Rock

ice from the river during frosty weather and store it in the Ice House to be used later in Donard Lodge. Ice was also brought from the lake at Castlewellan, where there is another ice house. Recent warm winters would suggest that natural ice would be hard to come by but bear in mind that a century and a half ago, it was much colder.

One day, I was sitting looking across at the Ice House with Charly, when a French female student came down the mountain path and asked me what it was. I explained as best I could and, after telling her that I was going to cross the river to take some photographs of the house, I invited her to join me for a closer look. "Oui", was the reply, though a little hesitant. After several clicks of the camera I suggested she take a closer look. "Non, Non", came the reply. It was only then I realised, that she was perhaps frightened of being thrown down the pit by this strange man and being unable to get out. "Merci beaucoup", she said and within seconds she was scampering back across the river, up the bank and off down the mountain.

Above the Ice House on Thomas's Mountain is an interesting cleft called Blackstairs, the site of a plane crash in March 1942. A Wellington bomber en route for R.A.F. Aldergrove encountered bad weather in the Newcastle area. The crew became disorientated, strayed off course and crashed into the mountain, which was obscured by very low cloud. Miraculously one of the six crew survived the impact. The fatalities also included a passenger, twenty-four year old Barbara Blakiston-Houston from Killyleagh, who is buried

The Ice House – not recommended by French Students!

at Loughinisland Church of Ireland graveyard, Seaforde. She was a Section Officer with the Women's Auxiliary Air Force. My recent searches reveal that not a scrap of the wreck remains.

Just a little further upstream, there is a wall on the river bank, for which nobody has been able to give me an explanation. The area between the Ice House and the wall is fairly level with a deep pool and flat granite slabs opposite. I can only guess that it was built as part of a picnic site for the estate workers and their families, at the time the Ice House was constructed.

The next stretch is fairly easy going, though you do need to watch your footing as you negotiate some stony sections and a few streams. The National Trust is also responsible for building and maintaining the stone paths that you will meet along the way. The method used for this type of pathwork is called 'stone pitching', which is similar to that used in the Lake District in Cumbria, England.

The Rocky Road to Donard

As I walk along with my staff, given to me by an old gentleman farmer in Wiltshire when I opened his local fête, I can't help reflecting on St. Donard who walked this way and wonder what the area looked like centuries ago. His real name was Domengard and he was a local chieftain who was converted by Saint Patrick. With Eagle Rock looming up on the left he would, as the name suggests, certainly have seen eagles in this locality. The advent of gunpowder saw the last of these magnificent birds removed from the landscape a couple of centuries ago. Meadow pipits can be seen all the year round in the Mournes but there are also skylarks and wheatears in spring and summer, with wheatears arriving as early as late March and a lucky bird watcher might catch a glimpse of a ring ouzel on the slopes of Eagle Rock. Known as the mountain blackbird, ring ouzels have a white bib to distinguish them from the more common blackbird. These sensible birds winter along the Mediterranean.

On the right flank, Slievenamaddy, Shan Slieve and Slieve Commedagh rise as the Glen River diminishes to nothing more than a trickle. Here you cross the river for the last time and start the steep climb to the saddle between Donard and Commedagh, where you set eyes, for the first time, on the Mourne Wall. The wall provides excellent shelter from the wind and is an ideal spot for a much deserved rest and refreshments. The Mourne Wall is 22 miles long and was built between 1904 and 1922 by the Belfast Water Commissioners to encompass the catchment area for the Silent Valley Reservoir. Peering over the wall reveals magnificent views down the Annalong Valley with Slieve Beg, Cove Mountain and Slievelamagan prominent on the right and it is instantly obvious that the climb was well worth the effort. The Mourne Wall is listed but this was no protection during the Boxing Day storm of 1998 when several sections of the wall on

The Mourne Wall, good for sheltering from the wind...

....except in extreme conditions when the wind can move stones!

Slieve Donard were blown over.

As mountains go the Mournes are relatively young and consist mostly of granite magma that rose up and then cooled some 50 million years ago. Successive ice-ages, the last of which retreated 10 thousand years ago, have significantly modified the mountains. Centuries of weathering have also contributed to altering the landscape to what we see today. In more recent times man has also made a contribution with farming, quarrying, reservoir construction and wall building. For many of us, the only knowledge we have of the ice-age comes from text books but these walks provide a real treat, as you get to see its effects at first hand. A saddle is a gap or col connecting two peaks of a mountain range and the one between Donard and Commedagh was created by the immense power of glaciers.

Many people come as far as the saddle and then turn back but for the more energetic the ascent of Slieve Donard now beckons. I never rush this climb, just put my head down, follow the wall and the last section to the water tower on the summit is easily accomplished. Mind you, there is a point when you think you are almost there, only to be disappointed to find there is still some way to go!

The lintel above the entrance to the Slieve Donard tower has inscribed upon it the date 1910. There is a notice saying Belfast Water Works, Trespassers Prosecuted and on top there is a metal plate used for triangulation (a technique for accurately measuring a large distance or locating a position

Donard's summit cairn and water tower

The view across the Mournes from the top of Slieve Donard

by dividing a region into a network of large triangles). The number 3087 below the arrow is a reference number, not a measurement of height. Along the whole length of the Mourne Wall there are only two other towers, one on Slieve Commedagh and the other on Slieve Meelmore.

A nearby cairn marks the exact summit but unfortunately there is little or no evidence of Saint Donard. There was once an oratory or prayer cell here but it was destroyed in 1825 by sappers of the Royal Engineers during the

St. Donard's Cairn

triangulation of Ireland. All that is left is a hole in the ground. Legend has it that a cave on the shore stretches the whole way up to the top of Slieve Donard and that Saint Donard's body is concealed there awaiting the end of the world, when he will re-appear. Donard, who frequently lived as a hermit on the mountain, realised that the actual summit wasn't visible from the land below, so he built a second cairn, where he celebrated mass. Local folk would know

when he was in residence by the smoke of his fire and would bring him supplies. Many centuries ago this mountain was a place of pilgrimage. While few who climb to the summit nowadays would admit to being a pilgrim, I would suggest in many ways they are. Surely one can't help being moved, if not by the whole experience of following in the footsteps of the famous saint, then by the awesome beauty of the place. Saint Donard died on 24th March in the year 506 but for some reason his feast day is celebrated on 25th July, the feast of Saint James. Anyone climbing Slieve Donard on that date may choose to remember both saints. Coincidentally it is also my wife's birthday.

I always advise walkers to make this climb on a day when a cold front has passed by with a ridge of high pressure following. This sequence of weather clears away the poor conditions and replaces it with clear polar air and excellent visibility. If you catch it just right you can see over a hundred miles with the mountains of Donegal, Wicklow , Cumbria and South -west Scotland coming into view. The Isle of Man to

A perfect example of changeable weather in the Mournes – always take care.

the east is especially prominent on such days.

When the weather conditions are right, para-gliders launch themselves from the top of Donard and land on the beach or in Donard Park but I have always stuck to walking for the descent. Care is required on the return journey as the loose gravel in places can lead to the occasional slip. Sometimes I feel I have done enough and simply retrace the route back along the Glen River to Newcastle but, if I am feeling up to it and want to make the most of the day, an alternative return journey via Slieve Commedagh makes a more interesting descent. The climb to the top of Slieve Commedagh is a little easier and shorter than Slieve Donard and in addition you can boast of having climbed the twin peaks of Donard and Commedagh on the one day. To reach the summit you first aim for the water tower before making for the small cairn that marks the summit. The average walker in the Mournes is unlikely to be under the same constraints as the Everest climbers, who literally have only a few minutes on top before approaching darkness, exhaustion and a lack of oxygen mean they must get back to camp if they are to survive. So I always spend some time savouring the achievement, whilst taking in yet more stunning views.

Having come so far there is always a tinge of sadness as one heads for home along the ridge of Shan Slieve towards Slievenamaddy. Shan Slieve overlooks the Pot of Polgarve which is a fine example of a cirque, a circle or amphitheatre created during the ice-age. The scree slopes below are a favourite feeding spot for the beautiful snow bunting. These little white birds breed in the Arctic and are one of the few winter visitors to the High Mournes.

A wooden stile leads you to a fire break in Donard Wood where the forest path will bring you back to Sonny's Bridge. The gradient of the Glen River path is such that you reach Donard Park in double quick time from where you can gaze back with satisfaction at your achievement.

Donard Wood

I consider Donard Wood to be an extension of my back garden, especially during the winter months when I can have it virtually all to myself. The wood is mostly conifers and, while it still belongs to the Annesleys, it is leased to the Forestry Service. A small area between King Street and Donard Park, known as the Annesley Demesne, provides a completely different habitat of deciduous trees and bushes, though it has been badly neglected for some years. Since the demesne was first planted in the early 1830s, some of the trees have died, while the laurel and rhododendron have been allowed to run riot. Nevertheless, many of the mature trees are still very impressive, such as the oaks, beech, yew, chestnut, cedar, tulip, arbutus (strawberry tree) and chile pine (monkey puzzle tree). Some time ago a retired botanist, who was scouting the area prior to leading a walk, inquired if I knew where the

A back garden extension to cause envy!

arbutus tree was. "The last time I saw it was thirty years ago" she said. I was unable to help her for, to tell the truth, I didn't know what an arbutus tree looked like but as luck

17

would have it, a friend pointed one out to me a few months later and even in January it was still supporting a few small red berries. Anyone interested in trees could spend several days here just identifying the many different species as I have counted five different types of oak alone. The demesne also contains a myriad of wildlife, not always evident when you take a stroll during daylight hours. Apart from the red squirrels, foxes, badgers, stoats, rabbits, bats, and the rouge fallow deer, it's the birds that tend to catch the eye. Among the more unusual are jays, long-tailed tits, blackcaps, grey wagtails, spotted flycatchers and tree creepers. Sparrowhawks and peregrine falcons are occasional visitors looking for a tasty wood pigeon. A wide variety of fungi, wild flowers, mosses and ferns can also be found.

This walk starts at King Street, near the entrances to Shimna Integrated College and All Children's Integrated Primary School, opposite a neat stone cottage that was the

The old gate lodge

original gate lodge to the demesne. Nowadays, the cottage is a private dwelling that has been tastefully restored and extended. The river to the left is Amy's River, which has its origin on Thomas's Mountain, the same river you see so vividly from the promenade, spilling as a waterfall into the quarry after a spell of heavy rain. In my younger days, a large corrugated iron gate protected the privacy of this entrance to the demesne but with the removal of the gate, the path now provides pedestrian access and a shortcut to town via Donard Park.

The main path through the demesne is called The Avenue, while another less obvious path to the right is known as the Back Road. Every so often you can see some cobblestones. These are in fact the remnants of the drains made from round stones gathered from the shore.

When I returned to live in Newcastle in 1994, the first thing that hit me was the sight of the huge amount of litter that had accumulated over the years since the public had gained easy access to the demesne. It had seemingly become a focal point for illegal campers and drink and glue sniffing parties, as tin cans, plastic bottles, glass bottles, broken glass and packaging of all sorts proliferated. I decided to try and clear some of the litter away but it soon became evident that this was no easy clean up operation; it was going to take some considerable time. In fact, it took three and a half years to clean up the demesne and I am grateful for the assistance given by Belfast Royal Academy, who help clean up the Mournes every year as part of their Duke of Edinburgh Award. The Mourne Country Centre, now the Mourne Heritage Trust, together with the local councils, provided materials and assistance.

A clearing of sorts just before Donard Bridge pinpoints the frontage of the original site of Donard Lodge, which has now been reclaimed by Mother Nature. There was some talk of the lodge being rebuilt but planning permission was not

Donard Lodge in all its
former glory
Sketch courtesy of
Lorna Stevenson

LRS

granted. The lodge was designed and built by John Lynn in 1830 for William Richard Annesley, the 3rd Earl, and a curvilinear conservatory was added in 1832. The lodge had wonderful views across Dundrum Bay, though today this is obscured by trees. The 3rd Earl died in 1838 and the following year hurricane force winds swept across Ireland on the 6th and 7th of January, causing extensive damage. This was known as 'The Big Wind of 1839', the wind that reputedly blew the fairies out of Ireland. The lodge and the demesne were badly affected. The estate was then managed by trustees and the main trustee, the Rev. J. R. Moore, began improving the grounds with paths, grottoes, rockeries etc. He was also responsible for building the road up to the quarries on Millstone and Thomas's Mountain.

A small selection of the varied flora and fauna found in Donard Wood

Priscilla Cecilia, Countess Annesley was the last Annesley to live at Donard Lodge, dying there in 1891. During the Second World War the lodge was occupied by the Americans but was so badly damaged by a fire that it was considered no longer fit for habitation. Subsequent vandalism rendered the property so unsafe that on 18th September 1966 the lodge was blown up by the British Army at the request of Gerald Annesley. The charges were laid on the 17th but unknown to the army the building was often inhabited by young people sleeping rough. Prior to action on the day itself, Gerald Annesley asked the officer in charge to check the building before blowing it up and so averted a terrible

tragedy, as some thirty youngsters and their belongings were removed from the lodge just minutes before it was levelled to the ground.

More recently the former lodge site was ear-marked to be the terminus of the funicular railway, that was proposed to run to the quarry on Thomas's Mountain. Local people, including myself, vigorously campaigned against this idea in 1996 and when the National Trust withdrew their support that was the end of the matter. While much was made of the fact that the railway would be a burden on the rates and it would become a white elephant, I believe the negative environmental impact would have been even greater. The demesne, despite its lack of management is a gem worthy of preservation. Woodland habitats don't just happen overnight, it takes many years to create them but they can be destroyed in days when the developers move in.

Virtually all the follies in the demesne have succumbed to neglect but one grotto still stands intact so before crossing Donard Bridge it's well worth taking a quick detour to see it. The grotto is located a short distance along the next forest path up and about 100 yards beyond a steel barrier gate. The design suggests it was used for picnics and the inscription on the stone above the entrance tells us it was built in 1842.

The Grotto

On the return to Donard Bridge there is a notice board on the other side which shows the route over the next mile as far as the quarry, following the road originally laid out by the Rev. Moore. The road takes you past three dwellings: a modernised bungalow, a more rustic woodcutter's cottage with an old Nissen hut in the garden and, some distance further on, a lone cottage known as Shepherd's Lodge which has recently been acquired by the Boys' Brigade. Much of the pine has been harvested in this area and has been replaced with mixed woodland. I was told by a reliable source, that a pine marten had been seen in this area in recent years. Known as 'tree weasels', pine martens are very secretive and only come out to hunt at dusk.

From Shepherd's Lodge it is mostly uphill until you reach the tarmac road leading to Drinnahilly and its radio mast. The road becomes very steep as you near the summit. I recently came up here during a gale and wondered at the fact I could hear a jet engine flying low. Once at the top I realised the noise was caused by strong wind blowing through the mast. To prevent myself being blown over I had to drop onto all fours. However, I thoroughly recommend this spot with its panoramic view as a stopping point. On Sunday afternoons in the summer you can sit and watch the yachts racing in the bay below.

Hidden from view on the western slopes of Drinnahilly is a large stone tower which forms part of the Mourne Aqueduct carrying water to Belfast. The tower was probably built as an air shaft and to give access for maintenance. I have been told

Radio mast and part time jet engine impersonator at Drinnahilly

by different sources, that the tower once supported large mirrors, which reflected the sunrise over Dundrum Bay into Countess Annesley's room at Castlewellan Castle – how fascinating and clever if this were true! A local man told me he visited the tower some fifty years ago with his friends and lit a fire inside. Within minutes the police arrived and they were apprehended. The tower is blocked up nowadays.

From Drinnahilly the next panoramic viewpoint, the quarry on Thomas's Mountain, is clearly in view. Sonny's Bridge is a good place to observe the habitat of the coal tits and firecrests that chatter as they skip across the tree-tops. Although the notice board at Donard Bridge mentions crossbills, I have to admit I've not seen one but that doesn't mean they're not here, so I'll keep on looking!

The quarry which now belongs to the National Trust is still operational, though this may change as the Trust has plans to enhance the area. The granite stone for the millennium

Amy's River flowing through the quarry on Thomas's Mountain

project at Delamont Park, near Killyleagh was extracted from here in 1998. When in place overlooking Strangford Lough it will be the tallest standing stone in Ireland. If blasting is in progress the route is blocked at Sonny's Bridge necessitating a detour via the Glen River, the mountain gate, the Ice House and up Thomas's Mountain, all the while staying well clear of the quarry.

However, assuming blasting is not in progress, it is well worth going through the quarry as the waterfall cascading down the rock face gives the place a beauty of its own. This is Amy's River which we earlier passed at the entrance to the demesne. Here it disappears under the quarry only to re-appear further down the slope at a spot called Lindsay's Leap. There must be a story here but it seems to have been lost in the mists of time.

If you look carefully along the ledges of the quarry you may see a raven's nest. The nest is made of twigs that have been added to over the years. Ravens are one of the earliest birds to breed, having their young in February. You would think that the blasting in the quarry would scare them off but they breed there despite the disturbance. Wherever you roam in the Mournes you will hear the unmistakable *'pruk-pruk-pruk'* call of ravens as they scour the slopes for carrion.

Leaving the quarry through the small metal gate to the south the route takes you up to the back of the quarry and along Amy's River to the area between Thomas's Mountain and Millstone Mountain with Slieve Donard towering above. The summit of Thomas's Mountain is only a short distance away and from here there is a grand view of the Glen River Valley and across to Slieve Commedagh, Shan Slieve, the Pot of Polgarve, Slievenamaddy and Drinnahilly. Finding the exact summit of Thomas's Mountain can pose some difficulty, as what appears to be a definite hummock from Newcastle looks quite different nearer the spot.

The boggy stretch from Thomas's Mountain to Millstone Mountain requires attention but it allows a magnificent view

The essence of Mourne – granite , heather and blaeberries on Millstone Mountain

of Newcastle Harbour through the fire break in Donard Wood. The fire break was the route of the old bogie railway line, that ran from the quarry to King Street, carrying granite that was shipped from the harbour to Belfast and Lancashire. The descent from Millstone Mountain is steep and you have to pick your way carefully through the heather using any rough sheep tracks that you can find, whilst all the time making a beeline for the disused quarry site. A black iron gate leads to Drinneevar Ridge where plenty more evidence of quarrying can be found. Abandoned kerbstones still lie

awaiting transport to some long-forgotten destination. A quarry path leads down to a rickety gate back into Donard Wood but before going through I like to pause and take in the view to the south along Leganabruchan and down towards Bloody Bridge Car Park. The forest paths lead to a final gate and stile, past some cottages and down to the main road (A2), which is called Ballagh Road.

The little stream or brook running under a wooden bridge near the cottages is called Scrupatrick or Saint Patrick's Stream, the point from which legend tells us Saint Patrick threw his shoe a full twelve miles, known as The Twelve

Maggie's Leap - Maggie must have been quite an athlete!

Miles of Mourne. I hasten to add that these were Irish miles which, at 2,240 yards, are 480 yards longer that the English or statute mile, hence Patrick's shoe landed much further south than first imagined. In fact twelve Irish miles takes us to Cassywater Bridge near Mill Bay.

Before making tracks back towards Newcastle it's worth visiting Maggie's Leap just a short walk along the main road towards Bloody Bridge. I'm always wary of recommending people to walk along this busy road. There is no footpath so take extra care if you intend visiting the site. Maggie's Leap is a large crevasse in the sea cliffs, that a young girl allegedly jumped to escape the attentions of her suitor, or a bull, depending on which version you like best. Maggie was carrying a basket of eggs at the time and managed the feat of clearing the crevasse without breaking any. Access to the site is gained through a gap in the wall and is suitably fenced off. The cliffs along this part of the coast provide good sea fishing perches but do be warned, these are dangerous places and young children should be kept away.

Costa del Down

Newcastle looks very picturesque from the Ballagh and more than one visitor I have taken there has admitted to the "Oh! I'd just love to live there" feeling. After passing the

picnic site at the Blue Quarry, King Street provides an interesting conclusion to this walk, giving an opportunity to admire and compare the old and the new. Halfway along you will come to a grassy slope on the right called Bogie Hill, which overlooks the harbour. The hill gets its name from the little trucks that carried the granite from the quarries. This is the old Newcastle and the surrounding landscape bears testament to what was once a vibrant community in the days of fishing and quarrying.

About two thirds of the way along is South Cottage which was the cottage my parents owned and where I spent many a holiday. I wonder if my mother would have been so keen to holiday here had she known about the experiences of a former occupant who often saw the ghost of a Blue Lady along King Street. The large white house beside the electricity sub-station, just before arriving back at the starting point of the walk, was built for the 3rd Earl Annesley's land agent and local tenants used to pay their rents through a door in the gable wall.

Happy holiday memories

Murlough

The Mournes from Murlough Nature Reserve

The Mournes aren't just about mountains, the coastline should also be walked and enjoyed. For this coastal walk around Murlough I like to start shortly after high tide, say an hour or so, as this will allow me to complete the whole walk on the shore and maybe indulge in a paddle at the water's edge. When the tide is full out there are stunning views of the mountains not available from Newcastle Promenade.

The car park at Slidderyford Bridge, better known as the Twelve Arches, just off the Main Road, halfway between Dundrum and Newcastle is the starting point for this walk. It is a good place to take in an excellent view of the Mourne Mountains before setting off, as the route heads away from them along the hard shoulder towards Dundrum for the first half an hour or so.

moult and breed. Up to one hundred common and grey seals can be seen here. Mostly they keep to the Ballykinler side but if you come across them on the Murlough side of the estuary give them a wide berth. Don't be alarmed if you imagine you can hear people moaning for that's how the seals sound en masse.

Suspicious Murlough Seals

I had some fun trying to photograph the seals here as, having had the good fortune to find them on the Murlough side, I had to get Charly to lie down some distance away while I approached. My recent acquisition of a zoom lens, allowed me to take photographs from about 100 yards before the seals took off for the safety of the water. Charly and I watched them retreat up the estuary and make a beeline for Ballykinler, all the time keeping a watchful eye on us, the intruders.

There are several warning signs here telling you to keep out when flags and lights are showing at Ballykinler Firing Range but you are quite safe on the Murlough side as long as you don't attempt to cross over to Ballykinler. The danger lies in it being a restricted area used by the army and the waters are treacherous into the bargain. Several boating accidents have occurred in and around the entrance to Inner

Dundrum Bay, notably the Victoria in 1845, which sank after hitting the submerged wreck of the Frolic, resulting in seven men and nine women drowning. The Victoria was one of the few surviving boats from the Newcastle Fishing Disaster of 1843.

Just a little further down the Lecale coast another drama took place in 1846 when the first iron ship, the S.S. Great Britain, ran aground in a southerly gale. The passengers were carried off in carts used for seaweed manure. The S.S. Great Britain lay beached for almost a year, before being refloated in August 1847. The great engineer and designer Isambard Kingdom Brunel came to supervise the winter storage of the vessel, staying at the Downshire Arms, Dundrum, for several

S.S. Great Britain in Bristol Docks

months. Apparently, it was on this visit that he caught the chill, which was later to develop into pneumonia, from which he died in 1859, at the age of 53. The lesson here is to wrap up well if you intend walking the shores of Mourne during the winter.

After a chequered career, the great iron ship was discovered rotting away in the Falklands. In 1970, the S.S. Great Britain was eventually towed back to Bristol, where it was originally built. It has now been restored and is open to the public. On South Promenade, Newcastle, you will see an anchor reputed to come from the S.S. Great Britain.

Dundrum Bay, and Tyrella Strand especially, was a graveyard for sailing vessels driven helplessly by stormy winds from the south or southeast. In the

S.S. Great Britain anchor on South Promenade

fifty odd years, between 1783 and 1835 some 58 vessels were lost here. However, the wreck of the Norse fleet on Dundrum Bar, around the years 923-925, is the worst recorded shipping disaster along the County Down coast when 900 perished. The fact that slaves were shackled to the boats, is probably the main reason for such a high death toll.

Many artefacts, such as elephant tusks, silver goblets and the remains of chains were recovered from the wrecks in 1815 and again in 1829. It's quite likely that many other artefacts still remain buried below the sands.

On turning towards Newcastle, the mountains once again come into view. It was Percy French who immortalised the area with his famous song *'Where the Mountains of Mourne Sweep Down to the Sea'*. Percy was born in Roscommon and his connection with the Mournes is a short and sad one. He married Ethel Kathleen Armytage Moore (Ettie), the sister of Priscilla Cecilia, Countess Annesley. Exactly a year later Ettie, whom he affectionately called his 'Little Ray of Sunshine', died in childbirth with the baby surviving her by only a few weeks. Percy certainly did visit the Mournes as he gave a talk in Kilkeel and he gave a recital at the Slieve Donard Hotel in 1915. However, it is less certain that he regularly called on his in-laws in Newcastle as Ettie's family were against the marriage. Surprisingly, he didn't write the famous song while he was visiting the Mournes but while he was staying at the Skerries, some 18 miles north of Dublin. On a clear day, Percy saw the Mournes in the distance and the words, 'The Mountains of Mourne sweep down to the Sea' kept coming to him. He went up to his room and wrote the song putting it to an old Irish melody.

As you continue along the water's edge parallel to the sand dunes it is a good place to beach-comb for interesting shells, pebbles, flotsam and jetsam while watching out for seals in the water as they're very inquisitive and often follow you

"Where the Mountains of Mourne Sweep Down to the Sea"

Sand martin 'des res'

around the bay and I once saw a flock of several hundred of the latter make a short stopover on their way north. The sight of seeing so many geese land and take off again was spectacular. Closer to the dunes you can see the sand martins, which nest in burrows there.

The beach here at Murlough was used as a military training ground during the Second World War and one can almost visualise the forces practising their landing manoeuvres. Here and there you will see the rotting remnants of Anti-Aircraft Landing Posts. As a young boy playing in the sand dunes, I remember filling my pockets with empty shell cases and bringing them home to my horrified mother. Replacement bombers and fighter planes were also stored among the dunes and Murlough Farm served as a landing strip. Nowadays, Murlough Beach is normally deserted but occasionally, just occasionally, along comes a long, hot summer like 1976 and the place is buzzing. Sun-bathing places are then at a premium with

Anti Aircraft Landing Posts

along the shore for some distance. I have a Canadian canoe, which I use in the bay when the sea is calm, and on several occasions a seal has popped its head up just yards away and followed for some considerable time. The canoe probably looks like a seal from under the water.

Porpoises also frequent Dundrum Bay but they tend to stay in deeper water. For those who are bird watchers, various gulls, terns, cormorants and guillemots as well as less common sea birds, such as great northern divers, razorbills, puffins and little auks can all be seen here. Gannets, all the way from Scotland and Wales are frequently observed crash-diving into the sea in search of fish. Mallard ducks, shelduck, barnacle and brent geese have been spotted in and the retreating tide leaving behind warm shallow pools for young children to enjoy. At such times you could think you were somewhere on the Mediterranean. If you just wish to visit the beach, then, from the car park at the Twelve Arches, you can walk straight through the reserve on the boardwalk to a point marked by a white post, which is about halfway along the beach.

From this point, Murlough Nature Reserve gives way to the Royal County Down golf course, which was opened in 1880. The course is protected from sea erosion by large boulders and rows of old railway sleepers. These defenses were extended and reinforced in 1998 after significant movement of the sand dunes. At the southern end of the golf course stands the impressive Slieve Donard Hotel, which was opened in 1897 by Countess Annesley, when Newcastle was fast becoming a booming holiday resort. The hotel was inspected in September 1897 by the Duke & Duchess of York (later King George V & Queen Mary) during their Royal Visit to the town. The visit of the legendary Charlie Chaplin in 1920 is celebrated by a bar in the hotel being named after him. Charlie used the hotel as a bolt hole from the world after learning of the death of his first love Hetty Kelly. The hotel has played host to many other famous people over the last century, notably: King Leopold of Belgium, Archbishop Desmond Tutu, Archbishop of Canterbury George Carey, Mary Robinson President of Ireland, Alan Whicker, Bobby Locke the golfer, Sir Alf Ramsey, architect and manager of England's World Cup winning soccer team of 1966 and football legend Jackie Charlton, manager of Ireland. I was instrumental in training Jackie's niece Suzanne as a BBC weather presenter. She is of course, the eldest daughter of Sir Bobby Charlton of Manchester United and England fame.

The beach in front of the hotel would have been a hive of activity in 1910, when 20,000 people turned up to witness the famous tractor manufacturer, Harry Ferguson, take to the skies to win one hundred pounds for the first engine powered aeroplane flight in Ireland. After several attempts, Harry eventually managed to fly low level for 3 miles at a height of 150 feet along the beach. I seem to remember the beach being private here many years ago and a long wooden jetty from the Slieve Donard Hotel was provided for its guests to reach the water. Your map will probably bear this out, as mine shows the coastal path going round the grounds

Slieve Donard Hotel

of the hotel and coming back to the beach on the other side. Private or not, the decline in sea bathing and removal of the jetty has meant the public regaining access to this area. Nowadays, the residents swim in the luxury of the Elysium pool within the hotel complex. The trees and bushes around the hotel are shaped by the prevailing south-easterly winds, indicating how exposed the beach is, when the wind is strong from this direction.

Beyond the hotel the promenade which runs from the Slieve Donard Hotel to the Glen River comes into view. The most eye-catching building is the church of Mary of the Assumption with its green copper roof, the first round church built in Ireland. If the tide is well out it is possible to wade across the Shimna River, if not, then you have to make for the promenade and cross by the footbridge. Where the river spreads out at low tide, is a favourite spot for seabirds, geese and ducks, which come here to wash and preen themselves.

Newcastle Promenade

The brightly coloured Tropicana Swimming Pool sits beside the Leisure Centre as you arrive at Newcastle Strand. During the summer months the sounds generated by a seaside town with its tannoy systems, amusements, music and gospel groups are clearly heard as you pass by at the water's edge. The once famous 'Pierrots' on the Central Promenade used to entertain the summer crowds here. I once plucked up the courage to go on stage with the famous hypnotist Edwin Heath who died early in 1999. He didn't have much luck with me. "You're too nervous" he said, "Please leave the stage". To be honest I was glad as I didn't want to act the idiot in front of so many people. Some years later he was instrumental in hypnotising my wife off cigarettes. She simply tuned into his wavelength when he appeared on television trying to rid people of the habit and from that day she was cured.

At the other end of Central Promenade is the Glen River where the spire of St. John's Church, perched on the hill, catches the eye. The church was built in 1832 by William Richard, Earl Annesley. The walk skirts around the rocks here beside the Rock Pool, which was built in 1933 and is probably the last open air swimming pool in the United Kingdom which uses unheated sea water. The pool has had its ups and downs but in its early days galas were a great attraction, especially when on courtesy visits the Royal Navy took part. There was always a flurry of activity whenever the Royal Navy, or the American Navy, weighed anchor in Dundrum Bay. The famous H.M.S Hood paid a visit here in 1929 before she was sunk in 1941 off the coast of Greenland by the German battleship Bismarck. These days, the Rock Pool provides a great focal point for local children and their parents during the summer holidays. At the end of the season, a swim from the pool to the harbour is organised, with the participants singing songs to help them forget about the cold water. I can vouch for the temperature of the water here, both as a child when I would be blue with the cold after a dip and as an adult, after being dumped out of my boat by a gusty wind. The site of the Rock Pool was once known as Ladies Bathing Place in the days of segregated bathing. Just beside the pool you will find one of the few remaining intact pill-boxes erected to defend the shores against enemy landings.

Heavily defended Ladies Bathing Place!

Just past the Rock Pool are the visible remains of a large semi-circular boulder structure on the beach. This was constructed for the Annesley family as a fish weir. After each tide, any suitable trapped fish were caught and brought to

Donard Lodge. At one time there were three such weirs on the beach, a smaller, less noticeable one, can be seen at low tide opposite the Strand. With fish stocks so low nowadays, I doubt if you would catch much there today, however, molluscs are still collected from the shore.

Oystercatchers in their distinctive black and white plumage and long orange beaks, are seen all the year round foraging between the boulders, while this is also a favourite spot for grey herons, especially during the late summer, when I once saw as many as thirteen. The street lights at night show them stalking the water's edge, then standing motionless, waiting for the next tasty morsel to come their way.

If your timing is right, you can walk along the last stretch of shore opposite the old part of Newcastle with dry land being reached via the Newcastle Yacht Club slipway just past the Harbour Inn. The North Quay was first constructed around 1820 and has been repaired and added to over the years. In Victorian times the harbour was a very busy place with fishing and granite exports the main occupations. Large schooners queued up and carried the granite far and wide. The Albert Memorial in London was built with granite quarried from Thomas's Mountain, which

Newcastle Harbour

overlooks the harbour. Nowadays the harbour provides mooring and shelter for leisure craft. Until 1993 the lifeboat station was situated inside the harbour where it had operated successfully since 1937 but a build-up of silt made launching at low tide virtually impossible. A new building was erected just outside the harbour, where the shore is firmer, and a new lifeboat, the Eleanor Girling, was part of the package to provide rescue services to the area by the Royal National Lifeboat Institution.

During the months of May to September, the Newcastle Yacht Club is in full swing with racing on Tuesdays, Thursdays and Sundays. I have always had a healthy respect for water but I overcame some of my fears when I retired here in 1994. I learned to sail with my daughter Shauna and shortly afterwards I bought a little Mirror dinghy. When repainting it in 1997 I named it Hale-Bopp after the comet which was prominent in the sky at that time. In the same year with my second acquisition, a Seafly called Ososlo, I did a piece for The Weather Show on BBC Television.

The last part of this walk leads to the top of the sewage station at the southern end of the harbour. The station is a recipient of a United Kingdom Tourism award and there are several reasons to come here. Firstly, it gives you a wonderful view of the route you have just taken, secondly, to show you that the coast beyond here is impossible to negotiate on foot and thirdly, to see Widows Row just to the left and a little further along South Promenade. These twelve pretty cottages with their dormer windows were built for the poorest dependents of those who lost their loved ones during the Fishing Disaster of Friday, 13th January 1843. Seventy three people from Newcastle, Glasdrumman and Annalong lost their lives, when a storm suddenly and violently swept in from the northwest across Dundrum Bay, devastating the fishing fleet. This led to the demise of the fishing industry in Newcastle, for legend has it that the fish, mainly whiting, disappeared at that time.

Throughout this walk your eyes will be drawn to the lighthouse at St. John's Point at the end of the Lecale Peninsula, some 8 miles east of Newcastle. The lighthouse, built in 1844, is 62 feet high and visible as far away as Annalong. The flashing lighthouse lighting up Dundrum Bay at night makes you aware that another world exists out there on the high seas.

Widow's Row

The Brandy Pad

Whin bushes in bloom at Bloody Bridge

Bloody Bridge Car Park is the starting point for this walk, which demonstrates that you do not have to climb to a summit to appreciate the Mourne Mountains and perhaps for that reason many people believe this is one of the best walks in the Mournes.

Before leaving the car park, I like to show visitors the cottage where Estyn Evans lived, when he was writing *'Mourne Country'*. He lived here for several years with his family, despite having neither running water nor electricity. From the bank above the car park the green corrugated roof

*Estyn Evans'
Cottage*

of the cottage is just about visible through the trees and bushes a few hundred yards up the mountain and to the right of the river.

'Mourne Country' is a masterpiece and if you want to read an in depth study of the Mournes, then I encourage you to obtain a copy. A Professor of Geography and Irish Studies at Queens University, Evans was, as you have probably already guessed, Welsh. I often wondered how he managed to put together such a detailed study of the Mournes, but all was recently revealed when I discovered that he had been a school inspector for the area before taking up his university post.

This walk could quite easily be called Smugglers' Way, as it was the route used by smugglers of yesteryear, intent on evading the coastguard or revenue men. Contraband, mainly from the Isle of Man, would be brought ashore along this coast, perhaps under cover of darkness, then transported on ponies across the mountains via the Brandy Pad to Hilltown and surrounds. Brandy, wine, silk, tobacco and tea were some of the most sought after commodities a few centuries ago. The role of the coastguard was very different in those days, when they patrolled the coast and checked every vessel entering port. From 1856 onwards, however, their main task became what it is today, one of helping to save lives at sea.

Now for the walk. Leaving the car park behind you carefully cross the road and make your way through the gate and stile. The plaque is a reminder that you are once again on National Trust property. Just below the sheep pens stands an old, stone bridge, known as the Bloody Bridge. This is reputedly the location where prisoners, who were being taken north to Newcastle or Downpatrick during the troubles of 1641, were slain and their bodies thrown over the bridge into the river turning it

Entrance Stile

red, so giving it the name Bloody Bridge River. It is hard to imagine such a dastardly act taking place at this picturesque spot but such is the troubled history of Ireland. Some more gentle folk say the bridge gets its name from the red flowers of the wild fuchsia that blooms profusely in this area in spring, summer and autumn. It would be a relief to think that this was the true explanation but, whatever the reason, prior to 1641 the Bloody Bridge River was called Midpace River. The bridge also provides an excellent platform to study the glaciated valley that lies before you. A lateral moraine consisting of boulders, gravel and sand laid down by a retreating glacier occupies the left bank. The river, especially when in spate, has eroded the side of the moraine over the years to form a cliff that displays a unique cross-section of its contents.

The Bloody Bridge

in summer, the bracken takes over. As you gradually climb higher you can often see stonechats with their distinctive orange and white markings. Their *'tsak-tsak'* call resembles small stones being knocked together. To the south lie Slievenagarragh and Chimney Rock Mountain, where the bare scar of Carr's Face is quite prominent and you should also be able to pick out the disused railway track to the quarry that once provided ornamental stone and foundation blocks. A small cleft on Leganabruchan to the north once housed a lantern, which was used to give the all clear signal to smugglers. The lantern was so placed that it could not be seen from Newcastle where the Coastguard Station was located. I once went in search of this small cleft finding a few likely candidates but left without any real conviction that I had found the right spot.

Upon reaching Glen Fofanny River, a plank and a stile provide a path across the river and you leave National Trust property behind. Huge water pipes cross above both the Bloody Bridge and the Glen Fofanny rivers, carrying water into the Mourne Aqueduct at the expansion chamber, located a short distance above and to the right. A retired geology lecturer from Queens University, whom I met when out walking in the Mournes, told me he once entered this chamber to carry out an inspection. The water was turned off and he was told that he had to be out of the aqueduct in Donard Wood by 3pm when the water would be turned back on. He was accompanied by an engineer but nevertheless it must have been scary.

If you come this way in spring you will be treated to a magnificent display of yellow whin or gorse blossom, whereas

Looking to Lecale across Dundrum Bay

The quarry is a good place to have a rest or to spend some time investigating the few remaining traces of the quarrying industry that once operated here. The four rusting metal chutes protruding from the concrete, carried stones of varying sizes from the crusher to the trucks. After the quarry comes the Bog of Donard and then the Mourne Wall. The bog is the source of the Bloody Bridge River and separates Chimney Rock Mountain from Slieve Donard. At this point you could bear to your left and climb Chimney Rock Mountain or you could tackle Slieve Donard to the right (in fact this way provides a shorter route to Donard's summit than that from Newcastle). This walk ignores both these summits but they illustrate one of the great beauties of the Mournes; there is always another walk to be had.

After the stile, the going gets somewhat more awkward as you head for the ford, where you cross to the other side of the Bloody Bridge River. Care is required on this stretch as the path is very stony and there is always the risk of a twisted ankle. If the river is in spate then rather than cross over, it is better to simply continue straight on until you reach the disused quarry. Up until a few years ago there was some heavy plant machinery lying abandoned on the river bed. The machinery was swept into the river during a flash flood, serving as a warning that heavy rain in the Mournes can, on occasions. be capable of causing a mini disaster. The flash flood here put paid to the quarrying and the plant machinery was removed from the river bed in 1997 by the Department of the Environment.

Donard Bog, the Mourne Wall and Slieve Beg

The beautiful isolation of the Annalong Valley

You set foot on the Brandy Pad for the first time after climbing over the Mourne Wall and, as you wind your way around the back of Slieve Donard, the whole of the Annalong Valley opens up before you. From left to right: Slieve Binnian, Slievelamagan, Cove Mountain and Slieve Beg occupy the immediate foreground and Slieve Bernagh the background. There are several paths in this vicinity, but for this walk I make sure I stay on the lower one, as the others are likely to take you off course and you can easily find yourself starting to climb Slieve Donard unnecessarily.

A little further along, below the saddle between Donard and Commedagh is some of the worst erosion in the Mournes with the granite crumbling and sliding down the mountainside.

Castles of Commedagh

The strange rock formations on the slopes of Slieve Commedagh known as the Castles of Commedagh are the result of thousands of years of weathering. Similar castles or tors can be seen on Slieve Binnian and on Dartmoor in Devon, England. This is about the halfway point on this walk, so a rest and a spot of lunch amid this impressive landscape is most welcome.

From here, it's basically all downhill starting with a gradual descent towards Slieve Bernagh, which is rather imposing with its bare summit and its twin North Tor. Just when you think you have seen everything on this walk, a second spectacular valley to the south awaits, this time the Kilkeel River Valley, where several feeder streams from Slieve Corragh and Slievenaglogh help swell the main river on its way to Ben Crom reservoir. Slievenaglogh still yields up small crystals of quartz known as Mourne Diamonds, especially at the aptly named Diamond Rocks.

The back door to Slieve Donard

*The Kilkeel River Valley with the Ben Crom Reservoir
in the middle distance.*

All too soon, the col between Slieve Bernagh and Slievenaglogh, known as the Hare's Gap is reached and this point marks the end of the Brandy Pad. This particular col is the best example of a mountain pass to be found in the Mournes. From here onwards, the smugglers would fan out towards their different destinations. Some say the gap is named after one of the more notorious smugglers called O'Hare but the less romantic explanation, and this is the one that prevails, is that it is called after a farmer by the same name, who grazed his sheep here. Perhaps he was one and the same person. I usually spend several minutes savouring the ambience, before passing through the iron gate and down the awkward, stony descent onto the Trassey Track. Slieve Meelmore with its water tower comes into view as the track is reached. Spellack on the left was well fashioned by the ice-age and provides a wonderful nursery for budding rock climbers. The climbers are difficult to see so scan the rocks carefully to search for them. The ford at the foot of Spellack is an ideal resting place to set yourself down on one of the boulders and if it's a hot day, have a refreshing foot-bath.

Another ten minutes or so sees you pass by some stone walled sheep pens and through the three mountain gates/stiles, onto the Trassey Road and the car park. This is where the walk officially ends but if you are up to it and there's light left in the day, you can always walk back to Newcastle via Tollymore Forest by following the lane above the car park. This is part of the Ulster Way and is signposted by the walker with a stick and haversack.

On finishing this walk which stretches from east to west, I always feel as though I have experienced the heart of the Mournes, while taking in the splendour of the scenery. Perhaps this is because the best views are contained within the mountains, rather than standing on a summit, looking out beyond.

...and its all downhill home.

Through the gate...

The Mourne Coastal Path

*The Cornmill,
Annalong*

I often take my grandchildren here, spending several hours on the shore, playing a variety of games. They absolutely love it and so do I for that matter, with all the entertainment free. I'm sure, if you visit, you too will be unable to resist acting out some of your own childhood games. Build a tower of boulders and knock them down with stones, or if the sea is calm, try skimming a few stones. It's very private down here, nobody will see you acting the idiot but then perhaps you prefer just to bathe your feet in the warm pools and bask in the wonder of it all.

Once more the walk begins at Bloody Bridge Car Park, but before setting off I often direct visitors to another interesting historical site nearby. Unfortunately it requires walking a few

St. Mary's Church – warning: can be eerie!

hundred yards further along the main road in the direction of Annalong to the heritage site of St. Mary's Church, which is on the coastal side of the road in the townland of Ballaghanery. You need to take great care here, as the road is very busy and there is no footpath. The chancel arch is all that remains of this early mediaeval church, which is thought to be one of the stations on the ancient Slieve Donard pilgrimage. The adjoining cemetery was used, up to and including the early 20th century, for the interment of unbaptised children and vagrants. I'm sure most people experience vibes at this one and an acquaintance once told me that a friend had a terrible experience here, when her guide showed her an ancient skull that he had found in the hedgerow surrounding the graveyard.

On retracing your steps back to the car park, you once again enter National Trust property by passing through the gate on the coastal side. The path takes you over a wooden bridge which spans the Bloody Bridge River. It pays not to be in too much of a hurry as the path drops quickly,

The coast beckons but every journey starts with a single step

otherwise you can miss the next turn and finish up beside the river with nowhere to go. From here onwards you meander around the rocky inlets or mini fjords, one of which goes under the name of Dullisk Cove. In spring, clumps of primroses and bluebells bring colour to the slopes and the occasional fulmar can be seen nesting on some of the inaccessible cliff ledges. After about fifteen minutes the path descends suddenly and you arrive at the shore in the vicinity of William's Harbour, which is one of the many places where William of Orange is said to have landed his soldiers.

You are now in the world of the smuggler. Contraband was smuggled mainly from the Isle of Man to these shores and just one successful trip could earn the captain of a schooner the price of his own ship. Smuggling was very hard to stamp out a couple of centuries ago as many local folk were involved with it in some way or other, but a certain Alexander Chesney, who was stationed at Annalong towards the end of the 18th century, took his job with the revenue service very seriously. In 1790 smuggling was at its peak and as you can imagine many of the smugglers were fierce men, who were very protective of their clandestine operations. Chesney was, nonetheless, determined to put a stop to it all, especially along the Mourne coast where smuggling was rife. His first encounter with smugglers involved a confrontation with the Morgan Rattler, which spearheaded several other well-armed boats in Glasdrumman Bay. Chesney's men tried to board and take possession of the offending boats but were repelled by a hail of bullets. Chesney, a prime target, was lucky to escape with his life while he was directing operations from the shore. It could be said he lived a charmed life as, in 1793 an attempt was made to ambush him but one of his staff, Alexander McDowell, was shot and killed instead.

By the time Chesney retired in 1822, extra manpower and resources were employed which checked the extent of smuggling activities, but it was never entirely brought under control until after the Second World War, when the laws on duties were changed. Alexander Chesney was obviously a survivor and lived to the ripe old age of eighty-nine. After his death in 1845 he was buried in Mourne Presbyterian Church cemetery, Kilkeel. In the 17th and 18th centuries this coastline was a hive of activity while nowadays you hardly meet a soul; how times have changed.

It is advisable to take this walk when the tide is out as several rocky outcrops have to be negotiated before reaching

....200 years ago, a clear moonless night ... was that the creak of a rowlock? ... the hiding revenue men hold their breath....

Green Harbour at the mouth of Crock Horn Stream. After leaving William's Harbour the route heads towards Portmore presenting opportunities to rummage among the flotsam and jetsam, or to simply watch the seabirds that fly along the coast. Grey herons scour the coastline, while the call of the curlew gives the place a plaintive atmosphere. You may also be rewarded with the sight of seals balancing themselves on small rocks beyond the low water mark. This area is a geological wonderland and there is a wide variety of flowers to keep any botanist happy.

Clockwise: Seal pup basking in the sun: Sheep's Bite and Hawksweed: Thrift on the rocks

About half a mile further on you come to Green Harbour and then, as you round Dunmore Head, you reach Glasdrumman Bay. Dunmore Head is a lateral moraine that has been cut off by the sea and forms the northern end of a raised beach, which stretches to Spences River. The raised beach

George's Quay

was formed after the ice-age had long since retreated. With the immense weight of ice removed the land gradually rose about 20 to 25 feet. Watch out for George's Quay a little further on, with its stony harbour and concrete jetty cunningly concealing a sewer. Jenkin's Point is almost unnoticed before you reach the most significant river on this walk, Spences River, which rises between Rocky Mountain and Chimney Rock Mountain. The route along this river was also used by smugglers on their way to the Brandy Pad.

Ships had no good reason to come close to this part of the Mourne coast. Nonetheless, the Irish Sea weather, in particular south-east gales, were still capable of beaching the odd schooner. In 1859 the Water Lily met its end in this vicinity, its final resting place being Glasdrumman Port, just a short distance south of Spence's River. A local fisherman, Henry Boyd, was awarded a silver medal from the Royal National Lifeboat Institution, for rescuing the entire crew of eight from the stricken brig. Other notable losses along this coast were the schooner Maria Lowther at Bloody Bridge in 1878, while the brigantine Sally & Ann in 1880 and the schooner Albion in 1881, both perished at Annalong. In January 1905, Dunmore Head claimed the tramp steamer Beechgrove. The Newcastle Lifeboat, Farnley, made several attempts to rescue the crew but gale force winds thwarted all attempts. It should be noted that the lifeboat in those days was launched by using horses and the boat itself was propelled by oars. It's hard to imagine the bravery needed to go out in rough seas using such boats. The crew of the Beechgrove were eventually rescued by the coastguard using their rocket apparatus.

A relic of Annalong's proud fishing history, now part of the Marine Park

Before leaving Spence's River the walker should sit down and look at the Irish Sea and imagine they are listening to the Shipping Forecast on BBC Radio Four. "Irish Sea, South-easterly, six or seven increasing gale later, rain, moderate or poor". Most of the shipping areas are named after islands, headlands or rivers, the Irish Sea being an exception. One of those moments that I will always remember was when I stood at Malin Head, County Donegal, as the Shipping Forecast was being broadcast. Perhaps I'll attempt to be on location at every Shipping Forecast area at least once when the Shipping Forecast is being read live. I would say getting to Rockall or South Uitsire could pose a few problems.

A shingle beach now brings you towards Mullartown Point where, on looking back, you get your first really good view of the mountains since leaving Bloody Bridge. Although Chimney Rock Mountain dominates, you will see from your map that Spence's Mountain, Blaeberry Mountain and the Long Mountain, stake their claims to the lower slopes. After rounding Mullartown Point on a grassy track above the beach you reach Springwell Port. From here the path above the rocks and boulders passes Arthur's Port and brings you finally into Annalong Harbour. The walk ends here but if you are not pushed for time you shouldn't rush away as there is much to see before you head off home. A large red fishing boat, by the name of Castle Bay, sits on dry land just before you reach the harbour. This is one of the interesting features of Annalong Marine Park and a tour around the harbour and the cornmill is also highly recommended.

Annalong Harbour has suffered the same fate as many of the small harbours along the coast of County Down, in that it is used mainly for pleasure craft, now that the fishing and granite industries have been reduced to a trickle. On a tour around the pretty harbour, you can't help wondering how such an awkward set-up could have been so successful, yet Annalong Harbour was for many years the main fishing port of Mourne, despite several craft being damaged during

The picturesque Annalong Harbour

desperate attempts to reach the safety of the harbour. Annalong Harbour became heavily congested when the granite industry took off. Mourne granite is the toughest in

the British Isles and was once in great demand; the granite quarrying industry provided much needed work for local men. Kerbstone known as kribben and square-setts were shipped to Belfast, London and North-west England. Some ninety per-cent of all Mourne granite, quarried between Newcastle and Slieve Binnian, was shipped through Annalong Harbour. As a young boy, I remember the square setts being removed from the roads of Belfast in favour of tarmac, as the tram gave way to the trolley bus. While much of the kerbstone stayed intact, the square setts were removed. Those lifted from the Donegall Road, were dumped at the edge of the Bog Meadows, where they were covered in clay to make a dyke, which went a long way to reduce the flooding in the area.

The cornmill on the mouth of the Annalong River was built in 1820 and operated up until the 1960s. In its heyday the mill ground most of the corn grown in the area. It was restored and opened to the public in 1985 and is now said to be one of the most picturesque in Ireland. If time permits a visit to the nearby Herb Garden allows a good last look at the mountains before calling it a day; Slieve Binnian, the large mountain on the left, is the subject of the next walk.

Slieve Binnian

Slieve Binnian

Ask anyone from the Kingdom of Mourne "Which is your favourite Mourne Mountain?" and a pound to a penny they say "Binnian". I feel a strong affinity for this mountain too, probably because my grandmother was born here, just off the Head Road in Ballyveaghmore. Slieve Binnian at 2,449 feet (747 metres) is the third highest of the Mourne peaks and the three hundred and sixty degree panoramic view from the summit of Slieve

Binnian is one of the best you are likely to see anywhere in Ireland. It is the most massive of all the mountains and is the only one to lie completely within the kingdom. Just in case you are confused I would like to point out that the kingdom refers only to that part of Mourne bordered by Scrupatrick, Saint Patrick's Stream just south of Newcastle, Slieve Binnian and Cassey Water and all lands to the east. In Celtic times a cowherd king called Boirche ruled this area from his stronghold on Slieve Binnian.

Slieve Binnian from Quarter Road

On the way to the starting point of this walk at Carrick Little on the Head Road visitors should stop for a while along the Quarter Road and allow themselves to be overawed by the majesty of Slieve Binnian, to take in the surrounding countryside and marvel at the stone walls made from the boulders left scattered around after the ice-age. The boulders have been set one on top of the other and together with the gaps between, give the impression of fancy lacework. The soil is generally poor, as it is throughout much of Mourne, and looking down across the patchwork of fields you can begin to imagine how difficult it was for folk to eke out a living from the land a century ago.

Whilst making a radio programme for Radio Ulster, on location along the foothills of Slieve Binnian a few years ago, we had the thrill of recording a cuckoo calling whilst I was talking. Folklore tells us, if you hear a cuckoo calling frequently, then it's a sign of rain. Take note that such maxims regarding animals, birds, flowers and insects fare poorly compared to those relating to weather elements and optical phenomena.

You can park your car at Carrick Little opposite the Old Town Road before taking the quarry track and heading for Binnian. During the holiday weekends this car park is full to overflowing, indicating the popularity of Slieve Binnian with hill walkers. This area was quite lively many years ago and I've heard it said that there were enough people living here to keep two Ceilidh dances going. Nowadays, there are only a few occupied dwellings.

Apart from the odd gentle incline the first mile is very flat. Within a few minutes you come across a field on your right with a derelict, two storey house. A cousin of mine told me that the Irish giant, Patrick Murphy, lived in this house and if I was to make a closer inspection I would see a stone

Giant Murphy's House

protruding from one of the walls, indicating his exact height. I did check this out but was unable to identify the stone that marked the giant's stature. There was however, an iron bar above the front door but as this was around ten feet I dismissed it, since at the time of his death, he was reputed to be the tallest man in the world at eight feet one inch. Paddy, as he was called, was born in 1834, in Killowen near Rostrevor and by all accounts he was very popular with local folk. He was reputedly a strong lad too, who smoked a pipe, which he often lit at the street lamp. He was persuaded to join a travelling circus and died of smallpox in Marseilles, Southern France, at the age of twenty seven. His remains were embalmed, brought back to Mourne and interred in Kilbroney cemetery, Rostrevor. Such was the physique of Mourne men, that folklore would have us believe that three further giants are buried in the foothills of Binnian. A story goes that one of the giants was always hungry, so hungry in fact, that he stuffed himself with hot soda farls straight off the griddle. I hope he didn't suffer from indigestion or heartburn.

A stile in the granite wall is provided for easy access where the path leads on to the mountain. Annalong Wood on the right still suffers the scars of a recent fire but looking ahead you can take in the magnificent views of Slieve Binnian, Slievelamagan, Cove Mountain, Slieve Beg, the Annalong Valley and Rocky Mountain which sports a roche moutonnee called Hare's Castle. A roche moutonnee is a rock shaped like a sheep as a result of glacial action. After

Annalong Wood

Slievelamagan

Annalong Wood you cross a stream, a tributary of the Annalong River, which is jointly fed by the two loughs we meet on this walk. I find it worthwhile spending a few minutes here refreshing myself as this is the only stream of note that you encounter.

Three interesting rock formations namely Douglas Crag, Blue Lough Buttress and Buzzard's Roost loom up to the left and somewhere hidden among this lot is one of the most difficult category climbs in the Mournes, or in fact the world, at a place called the Sheugh. These sorts of places are best left to the experts. Rock climbers in the Mournes years ago were obviously an intellectual lot as they gave classical names to the different climbs. Opposite the Blue Lough Buttress is a rocky outcrop called Percy Bysshe, presumably called after Percy Bysshe Shelly. It is also just possible that Shelly may have made an unscheduled stop in the area in February 1812, during his tour of Ireland. The ship carrying him to

The view from Percy Bysshe

Dublin was blown off course by strong southerly winds, possibly making landfall in County Down, from where he had to make his way to Dublin by road. If indeed Shelly did walk this way, then I can imagine him resting at this exact spot but it must have been an uninspiring day as no poem was forthcoming. Percy Bysshe Shelly, like giant Murphy, also died tragically at an early age when he drowned in a storm in Italy. It only takes a few minutes to climb Percy Bysshe where there is an interesting cave and once on the top you get an excellent view of the ground you have already covered.

The next stopping point is the Blue Lough which occupies a depression at the base of Slievelamagan. The lough, overlooked by the bare slabs of Slievelamagan, invariably looks grey to me when approached from this direction but I assure you it does look blue on sunny days. Slievelamagan's bare rocks were partly due to the shelling by the American Navy during the Second World War, when they used the area for target practice. Small bits of ordnance can still be found fuelling pressure on the Americans to come back and

The Blue Lough

clear any possible live shells. This pressure came on the back of the land mine clearances in Angola and Bosnia much publicised by Princess Diana but this needs to be kept in perspective, as I have never heard of anyone being injured in the area.

By now there is a noticeable increase in the gradient as you push towards the col between Slieve Binnian and Slievelamagan, where the wonderful sight of Ben Crom Reservoir and the High Mournes awaits. This is a good place to rest up, as the next part of the walk is fairly tough. Looking across to the other side there is an attractive stream with a waterfall entering the Ben Crom Reservoir and with this I want to try an experiment. Local people probably have a name for this river but nothing appears on the maps, so I am going to take the liberty of calling it Meel River, as it has its source at the foot of Slieve Meelmore and Slieve Meelbeg. It will be interesting to see what appears on the maps in the 21st century; will it be Meel River?

The ascent to the North Tor is the most difficult part of the walk with some tricky rocky outcrops to be negotiated. The path isn't always well defined here and it can be a bit boggy underfoot in places so walkers need to take care on this stretch. The rocks do provide wonderful viewing platforms but the slope on the other side towards Ben Crom is dangerously steep. The slopes of the North Tor is one of the few places I have seen red grouse in recent years as their numbers have declined significantly. The North Tor provides an excellent resting place and shelter too if it's windy. I recommend having a reasonable break here both to take in the view and to see if you can spot any faces in the weather beaten rock formations. I remember a Korean woman saying she could not recognise any faces here, only bottoms!

Stone shapes on Binnian

The Ben Crom Reservoir from the North Tor

Mourne erratic is Cloghmore on the lower slopes of Slievemeen overlooking Rostrevor. This huge stone was reputedly thrown by Finn McCool at one of his enemies!

Another rocky outcrop and a boundary wall are scaled before climbing and travelling along the ridge where you pass yet more small tors. The final ascent to the summit of Slieve Binnian is achieved with satisfaction. I did this walk with my son at Easter 1996 when it was sunny and cold, with wintry showers forecast. The northern sky became rather ominous as we left the North Tor, so we hurried along the ridge just making shelter behind the summit of Slieve Binnian before the cloud, snow and wind arrived. It was an exciting experience huddling behind the summit tor, eating our sandwiches, as we were enveloped in blizzard conditions with the temperature

From the North Tor one can enjoy the sensation of going downhill for a change. The small lough below on the left is Binnian Lough. On the eastern and southern slopes of Binnian there are several examples of the large isolated boulders called erratics. These Stranger Stones as they are sometimes called were picked up by glaciers, transported and then dumped miles from their origin. The most famous

dropping several degrees. Fortunately the blizzard only lasted ten minutes, the sun came out and everywhere was white with snow. By the time we returned to Carrick Little the snow had all disappeared, which just goes to show how changeable the weather can be in mountainous terrain.

Aftermath of the snow storm

summit and look down at the Silent Valley Reservoir, which is directly below. It's fun to take photographs of all the peaks by swinging round from Carlingford Lough in the south to Slieve Donard in the north. Having exhausted the camera it's time to explore the tors for faces as documented by Harold Carson in his book *'The Dam Builders'*. I have found several that weren't recorded; the one that looks like the gorilla, King Kong, impressed me most.

Before descending from Slieve Binnian, it is worth climbing to the highest point where you get an unusual aerial view of Wee Binnian, although this should only be attempted if you are agile and the weather is fine. By holding on to the metal post at the top it is said that you will be granted a wish.

When I have brought friends here for the first time I have found that, if it isn't already, their camera will be red hot by the time they climb up on the tors at Slieve Binnian's

The way down is through a gap in the summit tor and then along the Mourne Wall back to the quarry track and Carrick

Little Car Park. This is a fairly steep and tricky descent requiring you to pay attention to your footing so, if you want to take in the views, stand still for a few moments. This is the sort of slope that pushes your toes tight up against the toe-cap making for some discomfort. If this happens it is worth trying to walk sideways.

The Mournes abound in tales and Slieve Binnian is no exception. There are two stories about lights appearing on the slopes. One refers to an old lady and the other to a young girl who was defiled, murdered and buried on the mountainside. The lights are thought to be their spirits but perhaps a more acceptable explanation is 'will-o' the-wisp', a flickering light seen on marshy ground. To see these you would need to be brave and return here when completely dark but I for one wouldn't fancy walking here at night!

Tiring even for dogs

Silent Valley

The spectacular overflow at Silent Valley

The Water Commissioner's House

For visitors to the Mournes, a trip to the Silent Valley Reservoir is a must. To the seasoned walker however, the manicured lawns, flower beds and duck ponds set amid such beautiful surroundings, are in sharp contrast to the rugged terrain that lies ahead. Despite the artificial features, this area including the nearby Sally Lough, supports a varied wildlife. Once known as Happy Valley, Silent Valley is the name given to the area by the Belfast Water Commissioners. Some say this was due to the disappearance of the bird population once the work to build the reservoir really got under way in 1923 but in truth it always was a quiet place. Because of the geological difficulties that had to be overcome along this U-shaped valley, the dam was not finished until 1933.

The beauty of the Silent Valley is that it allows easy access to the heart of the Mournes and from the valley floor you can see several of the peaks, or Borkey Bens as my mother used to call them. Borkey is a name used in 17th century documents when referring to Mourne and may just be a colloquialism of Boirche, the Cowherd King, who gave the Mournes their older name of Beanne Boirche (peaks of Boirche). Although this walk does not take in any of the peaks, it is one of the longest, so most walkers will need all their energy to get back to Newcastle.

On leaving the car park and heading up towards the reservoir, you pass a pleasant coffee shop, as well as a good quality craft shop and a little further along you come to the Visitor Centre. Much of the history of the construction of the reservoir is on display there and it is well worth a visit.

Looking up the reservoir into the heart of the Mournes

The picturesque gardens of the Silent Valley

The area around the Silent Valley Dam provides a perfect example of the resilience of nature

The construction site, lying between Slievenagore and Moolieve was a very busy place all those years ago. Some two thousand local workmen were employed to operate the quarries, steam pumps and railway. Tragically eight men died during the construction. With so much going on in the area and the influx of so many people, a small town known as Watertown sprang up, just below the construction site on the lower slopes of Slievenagore. There was a cinema, dance halls, tennis courts, snooker and pool rooms, a police station and a variety of shops. A large coal-fired power station provided electricity for both site and town and probably for the first time in Ireland, the luxury of electric street lighting. The roads and hillsides were lit up in the early morning and evening by the workers lamps, as they made their way to and from work. Nearby Kilkeel enjoyed many years of carnival-like atmosphere, as the workers drifted in from Watertown. There is little trace of the site and town now, except for the foundations and ruins of the power station, shops and houses, which are mostly buried under thick scrub. By the time the dam was finished the surrounding landscape was devastated. It had become a wasteland of quarries, pits and deserted buildings but, with landscaping and time, the area has recovered.

I sometimes try to imagine the place alive with all those working men of long ago as I make my way up to the dam. They were a hardy breed who came to work and live at the Silent Valley, but if there was one thing that frightened them, it was thunderstorms. Occasionally, during the summer, warm, humid, southerly winds would bring violent storms from France. The noise of the thunder reverberating around the mountains, sometimes for hours on end, would test the sanity of any man. A particularly violent storm, one August afternoon, raged for hours causing havoc. All the metal equipment was alive with electricity. James Curran, one of the electric pump attendants, received a shock that flung him through the door of the hut when he tried to restart the pump by turning the metal handle. Flash floods from the heavy rain, washed away spades, shovels, wheelbarrows and timber. Thankfully, such storms occur infrequently but do remember, if you hear thunder, then you have survived the lightning. Thunder never killed anyone but lightning does and despite what you have heard, it can strike twice in the same place.

On reaching the dam wall, it is worth taking the opportunity of walking along its length for the views and to see the bellmouth overflow. Yes, the reservoir does overflow, especially after a wet winter and spring. The first time the reservoir overflowed was 8th September 1932; as the water level rose, a plague of rats that had infested the area fled to the high ground and tormented the occupants of the houses in the valley for years afterwards. The water running down the overflow and on into the Kilkeel River, is a really hypnotic sight. Before the dam was built, it was correctly estimated that the heavy rainfall in the area would provide 300 million gallons of water a day for Belfast. An underground pipeline carries the water some 35 miles to Knockbracken Reservoir, near Carryduff, on the outskirts of Belfast. Computers now help to check the quality, flow and distribution of the water. Fittingly, when the Governor of Northern Ireland, the Duke of Abercorn, officially opened the dam on 24th May 1933 it rained.

The tarmac road alongside the water allows you to cover the 3 miles to Ben Crom fairly quickly. Since Slieve Binnian towers over you your eyes are naturally drawn towards Slievenaglogh on the other side. Listen and watch out for the peregrine falcons that nest there. Racing pigeons using the Silent Valley often fall prey to the falcons. I once stood

transfixed here, watching a pair of peregrines calling constantly to each other, as they winged their way along Slieve Binnian and Moolieve. Please note that this Slievenaglogh, is not to be confused with the Slievenaglogh at Hare's Gap.

Shortly you come to the Slieve Binnian Tunnel. This two and a quarter mile long tunnel under Binnian, diverts water from the Annalong Valley to the Silent Valley Reservoir. The tunnel was constructed between 1950 and 1952. Two cousins on my father's side, Willie and Bobby Davey, moved from Belfast to work on this project

Slieve Binnian Tunnel – dug by Daveys!

60

and to this day they still live in the Annalong area. The tunnel was dug from both Silent Valley and Dunnywater simultaneously and when they met up they achieved the amazing feat of being only one and a half inches out. Willie Davey had the responsibility of drilling the pilot hole between the faces of the two tunnels. It was here, just above the tunnel exit, that I once saw one of the wild goats that roam the Mournes. It was well camouflaged against the heather and lay there quite still, chewing nonchalantly, while totally ignoring me. Wildlife in the Mournes is rather sparse and although I've yet to see a hare here, I have seen a common lizard. According to Mourne folklore, it's a good luck sign if a lizard crosses your path.

On approaching the end of the reservoir you can see three rivers on the far side. They are the Miner's Hole, the Shannagh and the Bencrom. As the road rises towards Ben Crom Reservoir, film buffs may well recognise it as the backdrop to the final dramatic scenes of the film *Divorcing Jack*. The geological and logistical problems of building this reservoir were nothing compared to the Silent Valley project three decades earlier, as it only took three years between 1954 and 1957 to complete. Climbing the steps, all 171 of them, allows splendid views from the dam wall and a chance to look for ravens on the cliffs of Ben Crom, towering over the reservoir which can store a staggering 1,700 million gallons of water.

The overflow from the impressive Ben Crom Dam

61

Lower Cove which has a dangerous cave. Casual explorers would do well to proceed with caution if they intend investigating further, as I have heard of people getting stuck inside it. The path makes its way past Cove Mountain and Slieve Beg with its distinctive feature known as the Devil's Coachroad. It gets its eerie name from the split in the granite and the resultant erosion that runs in a narrow ribbon down its face. You can see similar patterns on the slopes of Slieve Commedagh. The path peters out under Slieve Beg and rather than forge straight ahead to tackle the dangerous slopes that

After a break, the diagonal climb across the slope to the col between Slieve Binnian and Slievelamagan is a rather demanding stretch and you need to watch out for potholes. My record for this short, stiff climb is about fifteen minutes and I'm always in need of a breather here, before heading off downhill along the quarry track to the Blue Lough.

Skirting around the lough, past the slabs of Slievelamagan and across the heather, takes you to the lower path running parallel to the Annalong River. This path leads to the base of

would take you to the Brandy Pad, it is much better to follow the course of the Annalong River, up to the saddle between Slieve Donard and Slieve Commedagh. You may find this uphill stretch tiring but the saddle and the Mourne Wall are soon reached. I once met an elderly Norwegian trekker resting here and we got talking. He was touring Northern Ireland and was advised to take in the Mournes. On his first day it lashed with rain but he had the rewarding experience of rescuing a group of girls who had become disorientated when the cloud lowered. His second day, and

Slieve Beg and the Devil's Coach Road

The Black Ditch by the men who built it. Work on this project started in 1904 and took eighteen years to complete. In order to safeguard the purity of the water, no habitation is allowed within the catchment area; apart from the grazing of sheep, all other forms of farming, camping and water sports are prohibited.

Walking the length of the 22 mile Mourne Wall over 15 summits has always been popular. In 1957 the Youth Hostel Association of Northern Ireland (YHANI) inaugurated this walk as an annual event and by 1981 the entries had reached a record 4,000. The numbers, especially if the day was wet, were believed to be causing irreparable damage to the terrain and into the bargain the logistics of providing medical cover was proving a bit of a headache, so the event was cancelled after the 1984 walk. The Mournes provide walks to suit all tastes but if you are a long distance trekker then perhaps the Mourne Seven Sevens Challenge Walk might be more to your liking. This walk, which covers the seven Mourne peaks which are

Clean water en-route to your tap

700 metres or greater, starts and finishes at Donard Park and takes place on one day every August. You can walk the seven

this is when I met him, was glorious. While he was full of praise for the Mourne mountains these were his comments. "Your Mourne Mountains are truly magnificent but you know what spoils it? That dirty, grey car park in Newcastle is not good; you should have a showpiece gateway there for all your visitors."

The wall is quite substantial at the saddle and people often ask how they managed to manoeuvre the large coping stones into place. Quite simply, a plank was placed against the wall and the stones manhandled into position. The Mourne Wall stretches for 22 miles, is 8 feet high in places and on average 3 feet wide. The wall connects 15 summits and was called

summits of Slieve Donard, Slieve Commedagh, Slieve Bernagh, Slieve Meelmore, Slieve Meelbeg, Slieve Binnian and Slievelamagan in any order you like.

The final downhill stretch, the view towards Newcastle from the saddle

I usually take my time to cover this last section from the Mourne Wall along the Glen River to Newcastle, otherwise there is insufficient time to appreciate the breathtaking vistas. If you decide to do this walk, it might help you to know that the shuttle bus, which ferries the less energetic visitors between the Silent Valley Car Park and Ben Crom Reservoir during the summer months, leaves Newcastle about ten o'clock each weekday morning. It saves having to organise your own transport but do check in advance at the bus station.

Slieve Muck

Lough Shannagh from the slopes of Carn Mountain

Slieve Muck is unusual in that it has three flat summits of silurian shale over granite. This is in sharp contrast to the dome shaped summits of Slieve Donard and Slieve Commedagh or the bare tors of Slieve Binnian and Slieve Bernagh. Shale, the original rock formation before granite pushed up, is a laminated structure formed by the consolidation of clay-like sediments.

If you complete the extension to this circular walk you get the additional treat of excellent views of the Middle

by a small cairn while the third is easily recognisable by its nose like shape. This is definitely a spot where you could sit for hours identifying various landmarks on the landscape, particularly if it is a clear, bright day.

Below is the White Water River winding its way down to Crocknafeola with a patchwork of stone-walled fields leading down to Mill Bay. A network of rivers and streams feed into the Little Kilkeel River and the White Water River as they flow past the village of Attical and Knockcree to the south. Down below and to the left on the peneplain (an area so denuded by erosion that it is virtually a plain) is a long white granite gravel track. This is an old drovers' road known as Lough Shannagh Track or Banns Road and it runs the whole way from the B27 to Lough Shannagh. Without too much difficulty I can always picture a former age unfolding before me.

After you manage to drag yourself away it's a case of retracing your steps back to the stile at the main summit and following the wall down to Deer's Meadow. This is the steepest part of the walk which is why it's best to tackle the walk in this direction. You need to take extra care on this descent, as the ground on this north facing slope is always very damp. The slopes to the right provide the source of the River Bann, which flows into Spelga, before tumbling northwards towards Hilltown.

Mourne water was always highly regarded, especially by the linen industry as its softness was ideal for bleaching. The River Bann gave Banbridge an early boost in the manufacture of linen. By 1772 some twenty-six mills were established along the thirty-one miles of the Upper Bann.

Spelga Dam rarely impresses me, probably because I'm spoilt with the Silent Valley and Ben Crom reservoirs, but the view from this part of Slieve Muck is very much to my liking. The stile at the bottom leads back on to the B27 at Deer's Meadow. Having taken a few minutes to get your bearings, you join the Ulster Way along the B27 for a while and then back to Spelga Dam.

Spelga Dam from the slopes of Slieve Muck

For those taking young children on this walk I suggest that you follow a shorter route by starting at the Ott car park and returning the same way. This will avoid walking along a busy road especially in summer.

Doan

A visit to Doan will take you right to the centre of the universe, as far as the Eastern Mournes are concerned and if you are seeking the more unusual views, then this is the walk for you. Whilst Doan itself offers wonderful three hundred and sixty degree panoramic vistas, the views from the top of Slievenaglogh, looking back towards Ben Crom Reservoir, are truly remarkable. You could easily use up several rolls of film from this spot alone. If you were to ask me where I place this walk for scenic views, I'd have to say at the top of my list. Hopefully this fact alone will be incentive enough to bring you here. Where's the catch I hear you ask? Yes, I'm afraid there is something of a downside, as underfoot this walk has more than its fair share of boggy ground to negotiate and for this reason I recommend that it is best walked after a dry spell of weather.

Canopy of cloud clearing Doan

The car park on the Trassey Road is the starting point for this walk. There is a small stone monument here dedicated to Cecil Newman - Friend of Mourne. Cecil was a civil servant and a planner by profession. A keen rambler and environmentalist, he was a founder member of the Mourne Advisory Council, which was swallowed up by the Mourne Heritage Trust. After the Second World War Cecil was heavily involved in the reconstruction of Berlin.

The Trassey Track is one of the most popular routes into the high Mournes and within fifteen minutes or so you pass the conifers and mountain ash and are through the third gate/stile, onto the open mountain. The track meanders for a short distance round a stone-walled sheepfold and then back to the Trassey River under Spellack, on the lower slopes of Slieve Meelmore, before ascending to the Hare's Gap and the Mourne Wall, flanked by Slieve Bernagh on the right and Slievenaglogh to the left. The gate in the wall at the Hare's Gap from this spot always reminds me of a set of bottom teeth with a tooth missing.

The Trassey Track

In a move calculated to confuse the newcomer the Mournes have several repeat names such as two Blue Loughs, two Slievenagloghs, two North Tors several Rocky Mountains and Windy Gaps. To avoid confusion, the Sleivenaglogh on this walk is the Slievenaglogh overlooking the Silent Valley Reservoir.

This is a long and quite demanding walk so I often take a shortcut by crossing the ford and following the path below Spellack which brings me to a point just above the quarry on Slieve Bernagh. This is another working quarry though only on demand. This route means that you have to cross the Trassey River once more and then head up the Pollapucha Valley to the Mourne Wall, where Bernagh Slabs rise steeply to your left.

Pollapucha means hole of the hobgoblin or mischievous sprite and it wouldn't be Ireland if the little people didn't crop up somewhere in the Mournes. It takes a good hour to reach the wall and most walkers take a break here as the next section to Doan is rather testing. A new stile has been erected here by the Mourne Heritage Trust. This was one of six stiles airlifted by a Royal Air Force helicopter during the winter of 1998/99 and put in place with the help of Mourne Conservation Volunteers.

Once over the wall, Doan, standing all alone on the peneplain in the middle of the Mournes, is immediately in view. You have to be prepared for some boggy patches as you bear right and skirt around the base of Slieve Meelmore,

Doan Summit

half hours and still in good fettle. The times I give here and throughout the book are only approximate. In the Mournes walk at a pace that suits you and that is both comfortable and enjoyable. I certainly always want to spend some time on Doan taking in all the vistas. Standing at the highest point, if you slowly turn the full three hundred and sixty degrees and then try it a second time – it will look totally different if the light is changing.

Slieve Meelbeg and Slieve Loughshannagh with another Blue Lough below. If the ground is a bit softer than expected you can take heart in the fact that the higher you go the drier it becomes, which is also an encouragement for tired legs. Arrival at the mid-point of Slieve Loughshannagh is the signal to head straight for Doan and although you still have to dodge around the odd bog burst this route is much better than taking any ill-conceived short-cut envisaged earlier.

Doan means fort and from the summit it is obvious why such a mountain carries this name. Despite looking rather insignificant from this approach, it commands a complete view of the Mournes not afforded by any other promontory. The boggy terrain is soon left behind as you start your ascent of Doan, hopefully reaching the summit in two and a

When you are ready to leave it is easy to pick the next target, the Ben Crom Reservoir. The descent from Doan needs to be taken very carefully, as the first part around the tor is awkward. The best way is to retrace your steps until clear of the summit, then veer to the left, gradually

Silent Valley from Doan

Shannagh River

breeding season. Pigeons and rock doves form the bulk of their food and with a capacity to dive at speeds of 180 miles per hour, the peregrine falcon strikes its prey with instant death.

From Ben Crom Reservoir the route now takes you to the Silent Valley Reservoir shore across the mouth of Shannagh River to the Miner's Hole River where you will see a pretty waterfall. The Miner's Hole gets its name from the Cornish miners who prospected in the area for silver and lead in the latter half of the 19th century, without much success I may add. It is also believed that the name Happy Valley originates from this time, due to the laughter and songs of

Ben Crom from Slievenaglogh

dropping towards Bencrom River and on to the causeway over Ben Crom Reservoir. From here you can see the water overflowing into Mill River and on to the Silent Valley Reservoir.

The second half of the walk takes you along the ridge of Slievenaglogh overlooking the Silent Valley Reservoir and provides the unusual and stunning views I promised earlier. Slievenaglogh is a favourite nesting site for peregrine falcons which nest on bare rock ledges, laying three or four brown eggs in April. These birds of prey are a protected species and walkers should leave them undisturbed, especially during the

the miners echoing through the valley. From the Miner's Hole the route starts climbing to the ridge on Slievenaglogh but without the benefit of a well defined path. Walkers need to beware, especially in summer, when the bracken and grass grow quite tall, concealing the uneven nature of the ground. Once on the ridge, a path of sorts appears but you need to be mindful here too as there are steep cliffs close by. With some of the best views to the rear it is worth taking time out to capture the scene on film to treasure at a later date. The

Silent Valley from Slievenaglogh Ridge

summit of Slievenaglogh is, more or less, where the Mourne Wall from Slieve Muck turns sharply at right angles. I won't apologise for saying once again that it is worth stopping here to savour the panoramic views, as these are quite honestly breathtaking and will quickly disappear when you cross over the wooden stile on Slievenaglogh and leave it all behind.

The drop from the Slievenaglogh summit is very steep in places and some of the boulders are very large, so care is needed to tack your way down until you come to the ruins of the stone shelters, once used by the men working the quarries. From here there is an excellent view of Crocknafeola Wood to the southwest and also the last stages of the walk along the side of Slievenagore.

The last stretch is again very boggy so it's best to keep to the wall. Eventually a quarry track going south which brushes against the Mourne Wall takes you through a gate, past a few houses and then on to the C314 opposite the Ballinran Road. It is now only a short walk to the Silent Valley entrance from where the well organised walker will have organised transport to ferry them home. On the way you pass a red Water Service gate on the left. This was originally the Back Road of Watertown, the town that built up round the construction of the Silent Valley Reservoir. Many of the men who worked in the valley lived here in wooden or tin huts. The late W. H. Carson in his book *'The Dam Builders'*, records how the people of the valley reminisced about their leisure time. In consequence many's the time I have put my hands on the gate, peered through

Back Road of Watertowm

and let my mind drift back to a time when the crowds queued up to see Charlie Chaplin farces hissing and jerking across the screen beset by flickering black specks, or tripped the light fantastic, by dancing an old time waltz to the accompaniment of a Jew's harp.

Slieve Bernagh

To complete my ten walks I have, in my opinion, left the best wine to last and it really is a spectacular one with which to finish. While Slieve Bernagh only ranks as the fourth highest Mourne peak at 2,394 feet (739 metres), like Slieve Binnian, it looks and feels like a mountain should with its bare granite tors. If you were just to climb Slieve Bernagh from the starting point at the Trassey Road Car Park, then the thrill would be over all too quickly, maybe only taking three hours for the seasoned walker. To make it a good day's walking and to allow you to experience much more of what the region has to offer I prefer a somewhat longer route along the Trassey Road and up to Slieve Meelmore.

Looking towards Binnian from Bernagh

Once again the car park on the Trassey Road is the starting point, only this time the walk begins along the road parallel to the Shimna River between Slievenaman and Slieve Meelmore. This gives a chance to experience the countryside among the foothills of the Mournes, something that hasn't occurred much in the previous walks. The Shimna Valley is very peaceful with its few attractive farms making a pleasant contrast to the open mountains.

After a good mile and a half there is a small bridge over a

The view south from Meelmore – surely one of the most spectacular in the Mournes

to move a few feet away from the wall until you reach the Trassey River. Thereafter it is necessary to keep close to the wall until you reach the stile beside the Bernagh Slabs. The gradient up to Slieve Bernagh is as steep as anywhere on the Mournes, so after crossing the stile I usually weave in and out to make the going easier on my joints, occasionally taking time to look back at both Slieves, Meelmore and Meelbeg, as this also gives an excuse to rest. Doan, Slieve Muck, Blue Lough, Slieve Loughshannagh and Silent Valley all stand out near the summit. Further to the south, Mill Bay and Carlingford Lough are clearly visible on most days.

The Mournes support a healthy insect population and during the warm summer months, bees and even the odd butterfly will frequent the higher summits. It was no great surprise but yet a delight to see a red admiral butterfly here one warm August day. I guess it must have been sucked up into the mountains by the thermals that had developed. Red admirals migrate from the Mediterranean each year, though it's known for them to survive hibernation this far north.

Like Slieve Binnian, the summit of Slieve Bernagh has several interesting tors but unfortunately no faces of any great note. The tors here are much more pointed and difficult to climb so a word or two of warning; to climb a summit tor made of granite might be reasonably easy but coming down is a different proposition, as the footholds you saw and used on the way up cannot be seen on the way down. It is good to spend some time here on Slieve Bernagh summit, examining the tors and enjoying the views from its many vantage points and, besides, there's nowhere better to have your packed lunch!

Departing from Slieve Bernagh the route heads east, dropping all the while towards the North Tor. Some walkers might be tempted to give this tor a miss, but I can assure you that it is well worth the extra effort involved to take it in before returning to the path below and making for the Hare's Gap. I am always careful to bear off to the right on the final approach to the gap, as a sharp drop occurs here with the Mourne Wall suddenly vanishing. This could be a lethal hazard if following the wall down in poor visibility.

Tors on Bernagh

On the approach to the Hare's Gap you will notice some stones laid out like the foundations of a little house. I have it on good authority that this is the remnant of a Booley Hut, a makeshift shelter used by farmers. These huts were used in

Acknowledgments

I wish to express my sincere thanks to Bill Giles for agreeing to write the foreword and Lorna Stevenson for the sketch of Donard Lodge. I am indebted to my wife Teresa who tirelessly edited and proof read the various drafts. Teresa (who took the cover photograph), together with my daughter Shauna and my grandson Colum, helped with the photography. I would also like to thank the staff of Newcastle Library for their assistance, the Local Studies Section, S.E.E.L.B Library Headquarters, Ballynahinch, Belfast Weather Centre for statistical information, Terence Bowman, Editor of the Mourne Observer and all those I have met and walked with in and around the Mournes.

Appendix 1: A Brief Guide to Weather Charts

It is always a good idea to get a weather forecast before planning a hill walk. If you have some understanding of weather charts and what type of weather a certain wind direction brings then you are well on the road to deciding if a particular day is suitable for walking in the Mournes.

Some simple guidelines:-

1. High Pressure (including ridge) usually means settled weather.

2. Low pressure (including trough) signifies disturbed weather.

3. Isobars are lines of equal pressure. The distance between isobars is inversely proportional to the wind strength i.e. the closer together they are the stronger the wind.

4. Winds move clockwise round High Pressure and anti-clockwise round Low Pressure.

5. Fronts, whether they be warm, cold or occluded mean cloud and rain. Fronts are really imaginary lines on a weather map that show where two different types of air meet.

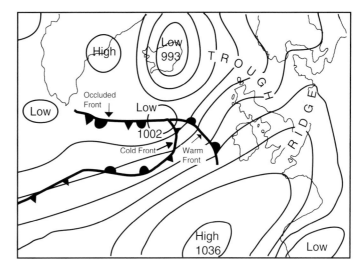

A typical weather chart showing most of the features described in the text

6. A marked change in wind direction usually means a change in weather type.

7. Northerly winds are cold, southerly winds are warm.

8. Winds that travel over the sea are moist, those that travel over land are dry.

9. Remember wind direction is where the wind is coming from not where it is going to i.e. a Northwest wind is coming from the Northwest.

Appendix 2: Bibliography

Belfast RSPB Belfast Group, Birds Beyond Belfast

Carson W.H., The Dam Builders, Newcastle, The Mourne Observer Press, 1981.

Corlett E., The Iron Ship, London, Conway Maritime Press, 1990.

Department of the Environment, Mourne Mountain Walks, Belfast, HMSO, 1990.

Doran J.S., Hill Walks in the Mournes, Newcastle, Mourne Observer Press.

Doran J.S., My Mourne, Newcastle, Mourne Observer Press.

Evans E.E., Mourne Country, Dundalk, Dundalgan Press, 1989.

Fitzpatrick W.J., A Mourne Man's Memories, Newcastle, Mourne Observer Press, 1980.

Hammond F. & Porter T., A Tour of the Mournes, Belfast, The Friar's Bush Press, 1991.

Healy N.J., Percy French and His Songs, Dublin, Mercier Press, 1977.

Krakauer J., Into Thin Air, London, Pan Books, 1998.

Lecale Miscellany

Marriot P.J., Red Sky At Night Shepherd's Delight?, Oxford, Sheba Books, 1981.

Morton G., Victorian and Edwardian Newcastle, The Friar's Bush Press, Belfast, 1988.

Mourne Observer, Sailing Ships of Mourne, Newcastle, Mourne Observer, 1995.

Newcastle Chamber of Commerce, Discover Newcastle, GCAS Publications.

O'Dowda B., The World of Percy French, Belfast, The Blackstaff Press, 1997.

Porter T., Annalong in the 1800s, Rathfriland, Outlook Press, 1997.

Research Siobhan Lanigan-O'Keeffe., ed. Niki Hill, Celebration of a century, Belfast, Tudor Journals Ltd. 1997.

Thomas M., Weather for Hill Walkers & Climbers, Stroud, Alan Sutton Publishing Ltd., 1995.

Turner A., Walking the Ulster Way, Belfast, The Appletree Press, 1989.

Twelve Miles of Mourne, Newry, Hollywood Printers.

Wilson I., Shipwrecks of the Ulster Coast, Coleraine, Impact Printing Ltd., 1997.

Appendix 3: Useful contacts for Walkers in the Mournes

Mountain Rescue Group
Newcastle Police Station
South Promenade
Newcastle
BT33 0EY
Tel:- (028) 4372 3583

Newcastle Police Station
South Promenade
Newcastle
BT33 0EY
Tel:- (028) 4372 3583

Mourne Heritage Trust
87 Central Promenade
Newcastle
BT33 0EH
Tel:- (028) 4372 4059

Newcastle Youth Hostel
30 Downs Road
Newcastle
BT33 0AG
Tel:- (028) 4372 2133

Northern Ireland Mountain Centre
Bryansford
Newcastle
BT33 0PT
Tel:- (028) 4372 2158

Newcastle Tourist Information Centre
Newcastle Centre
10-14 Central Promenade
Newcastle
BT33 0AA
Tel:-(028) 4372 2222

Weathercall (Northern Ireland)
0891500427

Marinecall (Lough Foyle to Carlingford Lough)
0891500465

Cottage

Publications

Dear Reader

We hope you have found this book both enjoyable and useful.

If you are interested in books and prints of Ireland you should know that in addition to this title we have published a range of illustrated books and artist signed prints. Each book is lavishly illustrated by a local artist and focuses on a specific area of Ireland, its history, people and folklore.

For more details on these superb publications and view samples of the beautiful paintings they contain, you can visit our web site at **www.cottage-publications.com** or alternatively you can contact us as follows:-

Telephone: (028) 9188 8033
Fax: (028) 9188 8063
E-mail: info@cottage-publications.com

or write to:–

Cottage Publications
15 Ballyhay Road
Donaghadee, Co. Down
N. Ireland, BT21 0NG